JOURNEY THROUGH

Japan

Richard Tames

Troll Associates

Library of Congress Cataloging-in-Publication Data

Tames, Richard.
    Journey through Japan / by Richard Tames;
illustrated by Martin Camm, Mike Roffe, and
Ian Thompson.
      p.   cm.
    Summary: An introduction to the history,
geography, culture, and people of Japan.
Includes a chart of key facts and information
on the population, education, and industry.
    ISBN 0-8167-2114-9 (lib. bdg.)
    ISBN 0-8167-2115-7 (pbk.)
    1. Japan—Description and travel—1945 - —
Juvenile literature. [1. Japan.] I. Camm,
Martin, ill. II. Roffe, Michael, ill.
III. Thompson, Ian, 1964-   ill. IV. Title.
DS811.T288 1991
952—dc20   90-10944

Published by Troll Associates, Mahwah,
New Jersey 07430

Edited by Neil Morris

Design by James Marks
Picture research by Caroline Mitchell.

Illustrators: Martin Camm: page 4;
David More: page 14; Mike Roffe: pages 5,
7, 11, 14; Ian Thompson: pages 4-5.

Picture Credits: Barnabys: pages 7, 23 (bottom),
30 (left); Robert Harding: pages 15, 17 (left), 28/29;
Geoff Howard: pages 9 (top), 20-21, 21 (top), 25;
Lydia Howitt: page 30 (right); Hutchison: pages
8-9, 10-11, 12, 12-13, 16-17, 19; Japan Information
& Cultural Centre: pages 9 (bottom), 10, 17 (right),
26-27; Japanese Tourist Organisation pages 13, 23
(top), 24 (top), 27 (bottom); ZEFA: cover, pages 1,
6-7, 14-15, 18, 18-19, 21 (bottom), 22-23, 24 (bottom), 27
(top).

Printed in the U.S.A.
10   9   8   7   6   5   4   3   2   1

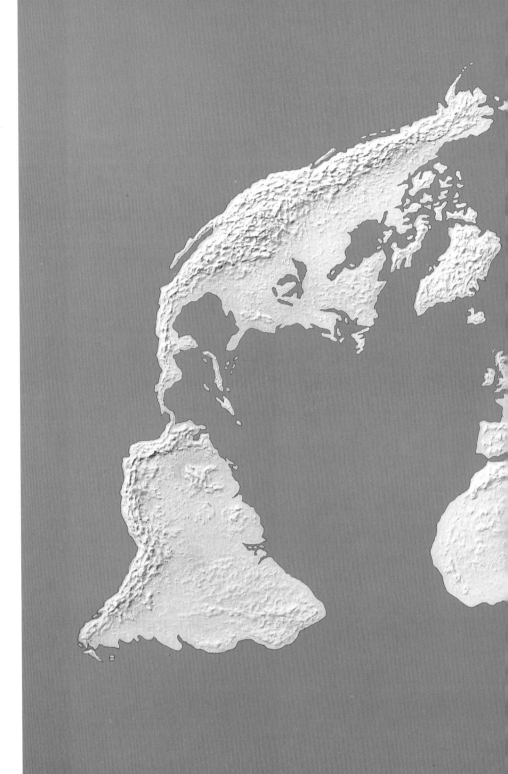

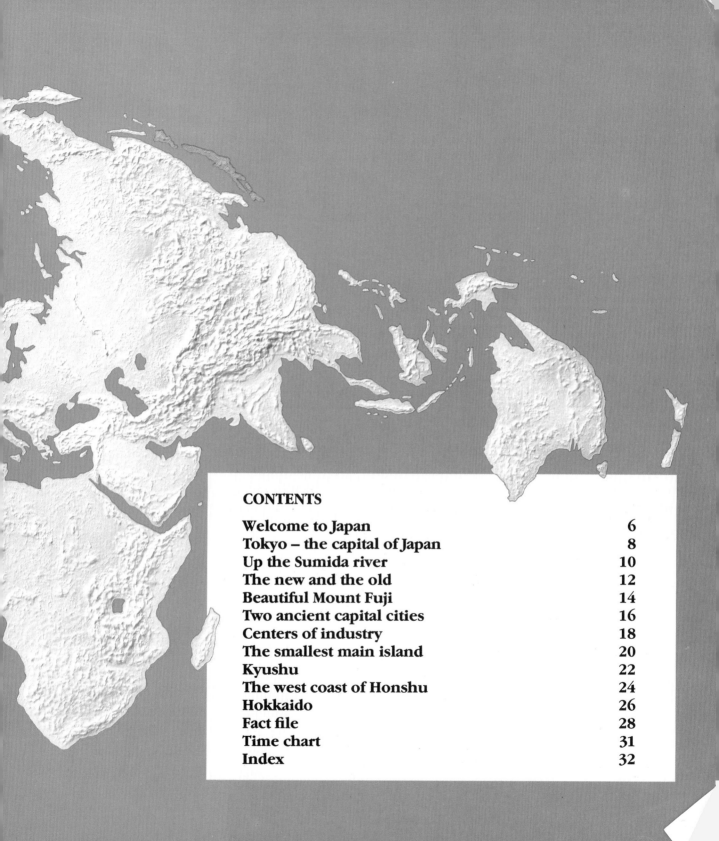

CONTENTS

Japan

KEY FACTS

Area: 377,800 sq. km (145,900 sq. mi.) – this area is spread over nearly 4,000 islands

Population: 123,231,000

Capital: Tokyo 12,524,000 people

Other major cities: Yokohama 2,993,000 Osaka 2,636,000 Nagoya 2,116,000

Highest mountain: Mount Fuji (also called Fuji-san) 3,776 m (12, 388 ft.) – a dormant volcano which last erupted in 1707

Longest river: Shinano-gawa 367 km (228 mi.)

Largest lake: Lake Biwa 674 sq.km (260 sq. mi.)

Cormorant

Animals of Japan
The Japanese macaque is a hardy monkey. It survives snowy winters. Some fishermen train cormorants to catch fish for them.

Japanese macaque

4

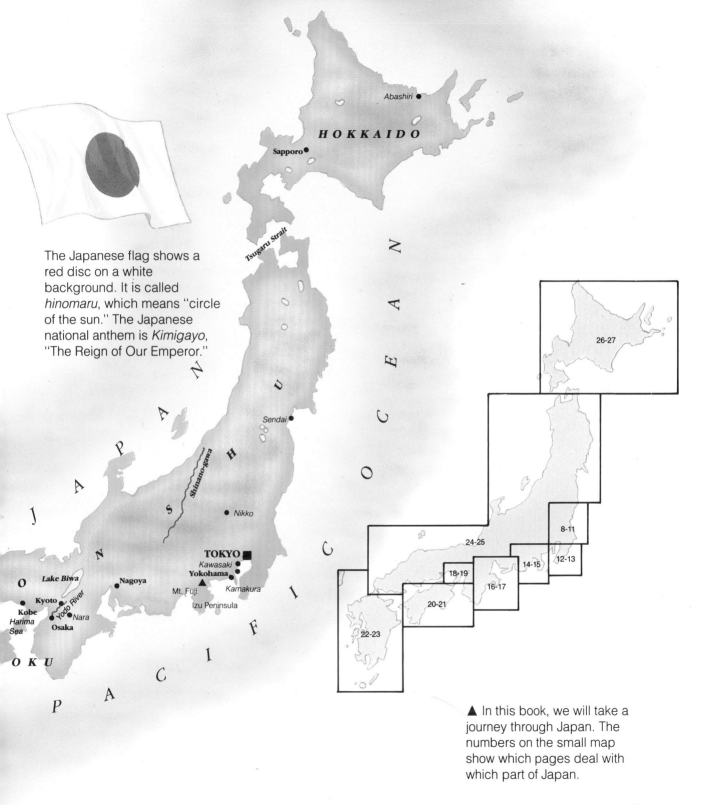

The Japanese flag shows a red disc on a white background. It is called *hinomaru*, which means "circle of the sun." The Japanese national anthem is *Kimigayo*, "The Reign of Our Emperor."

▲ In this book, we will take a journey through Japan. The numbers on the small map show which pages deal with which part of Japan.

Welcome to Japan

Japan is a chain of nearly four thousand islands. Most of the 123 million people of Japan live in flat areas on four main islands. These islands are called Honshu, Hokkaido, Kyushu, and Shikoku. About three-quarters of Japan is mountainous, and most of the mountains are covered by forests. There are very few rivers. Most of them are quite short and shallow, so they are not used for transport. However, there are a number of large lakes. Japan has over sixty active volcanoes and it suffers greatly from earthquakes. In Tokyo you can usually feel shocks about every three days. In late summer, Japan is often battered by typhoons.

The Japanese call their country Nippon. The English word "Japan" is a version of a Chinese word which means "land of the rising sun." The Japanese used to believe their country was created by tears from heaven.

Japan is different from any other country in several ways. Its language is unlike any other. Its writing is based on ancient Chinese characters, but it has developed differently from Chinese.

Over many years the Japanese have developed arts and pastimes found nowhere else. In the tea ceremony, fragrant tea is served according to special rules. *Bonsai* is the delicate art of growing miniature trees in pots.

You will see both traditional and modern ways of life in Japan. A man may go to the office in a western-style suit, but when he comes home he may change into a comfortable *kimono,* a robe-like garment tied with a sash called an *obi.*

Your journey through Japan begins in Tokyo, the capital. Tokyo is on the island of Honshu, the biggest and most populated island.

▶ In the Japanese countryside, hills are often terraced for cultivation.

▼ A shopping street in Osaka. Cities are scattered throughout the Japanese islands. About three-quarters of the people live in cities. Western-style dress is common, but some people still wear the traditional kimono.

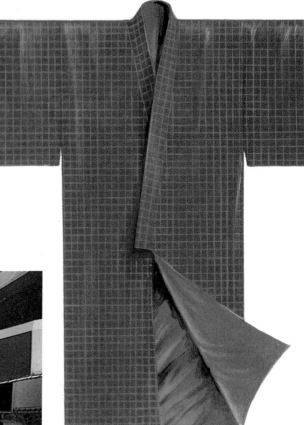

▲ The kimono is the traditional costume of Japan. It is wrapped over at the front, and tied with a sash at the back.

Tokyo – the capital of Japan

Tokyo is the biggest city in Japan and the heart of the country's life. It is the center of government, business, broadcasting, and newspapers. The city merges with surrounding towns to create an endless sprawl across the Kanto plain of over 30 million people. This plain is Japan's largest area of level land. Hills enclose the city on three sides. From Tokyo, you can see the peak of Mount Fuji, Japan's highest point, on a clear day.

You could easily lose your way in Tokyo. Very few Japanese speak foreign languages, but there are special yellow phones for tourists who get lost. During the rush hours the trains are very crowded. At some stations there are special officials whose job is to push people into trains so the doors will squeeze shut.

Tokyo is not a very old city. It was a small fishing village until the warlord Ieyasu Tokugawa built the great Edo Castle there about 400 years ago. It became the center of power in Japan. In those days the city was called Edo. A little over a hundred years ago, the emperor Meiji moved from Kyoto to Edo and renamed it Tokyo, which means "Eastern capital." The present-day Emperor's palace is built in the grounds of Edo Castle.

Few old buildings remain in Tokyo. The city has suffered destruction due to natural disasters and war. In the great earthquake of 1923, more than 100,000 people were killed or injured. Large parts of the city were completely destroyed.

Shops, offices, factories, and homes are mixed together all over Tokyo, but there are also districts that have their own particular character. You can visit Ginza for very expensive shopping. Akihabara has many tiny shops and stalls selling electrical goods.

▲ A scene from a *kabuki* play. In this costumed drama, all the parts are usually played by men wearing make-up.

▲ (*top right*) A "capsule hotel" in Tokyo. Each small room usually has a TV and phone. These hotels are mostly used by businessmen staying one night only.

▶ The Imperial Palace. The home of the Emperor is one of the few old buildings still standing in Tokyo.

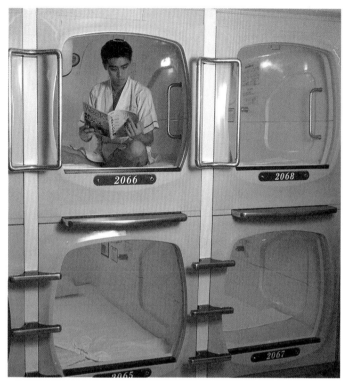

Up the Sumida river

One of the best trips in Tokyo is the river bus. This is a forty-minute ride in a double-decker boat that goes up the Sumida river to Asakusa. The boat goes under eleven bridges, from the Kachidoki split bridge to the Kiyosu suspension bridge.

From the river you can see the Tsukiji fish market. This is the largest fish market in the world. Early every morning, fish are brought from the coasts of Japan and are sold to the shops and restaurants. There is little meat in Japan, so people eat a lot of fish. They eat it either raw, as *sashimi*, or cooked. Heart complaints are rare in Japan because of the healthy diet.

You should also look out for the Kokugikan with its green roof. This is the main arena for sumo wrestling, where tournaments are held three times a year. Sumo is a very popular sport to watch. You can see the huge wrestlers practicing every morning. At the end of the trip is Asakusa Kannon, a 300-year-old building, the oldest Buddhist temple in Tokyo.

From Asakusa you can take the train to Nikko. Nikko is famous for magnificent golden shrines with intricate carvings of birds and animals. It is also a beautiful national park. You can drive up to Lake Chuzenji, which is so high that it is quite cold even in the middle of summer. At the end of July there is a festival in which local people float thousands of lighted paper lanterns across the lake in the evening. The Japanese Festival of Lanterns honors the spirits of those who have left this world. Some people believe that these spirits return once a year to visit their families.

At one end of the lake are the Kegon Falls, which are just over 100 meters (328 feet) high. In winter some of the water freezes into long icicles.

▲ People in Japan eat mostly rice, fish, and vegetables. *Sushi* are small rice balls with raw fish or vegetables.

◄ Sumo wrestling for the Grand Championship. This ancient form of wrestling is the national sport of Japan. A match is lost by the wrestler who first steps out of the ring or touches the ground with anything but the soles of his feet.

▼ A Sumida river bus takes over 500 passengers. On the river there are regattas in spring and fireworks in summer.

The new and the old

There are two contrasting cities to the south of Tokyo. Yokohama is a thriving port. For more than 200 years, Japan had no contact with foreign people. In 1853 an American naval fleet commanded by Commodore Matthew Perry arrived in Japan, and forced Japan to renew its contact with the outside world. The Japanese disliked these western "barbarians" and set aside a totally separate neighborhood for them in Yokohama. You can still see some of the English merchants' houses in the foreigners' area of the city. The foreign traders living in Yokohama soon built the small fishing village up into a very large, busy port.

Kamakura has a famous past and many old buildings. In 1180 the warrior Yoritomo set up his headquarters there, as it was a natural stronghold surrounded by hills and the sea. From here his family, the Minamoto, took control of Japan as *shoguns*. Shoguns were military leaders who ruled the country, while the emperors kept their title but had no power.

The Minamoto family were *samurai*. Samurai warriors were trained to fight with sword, lance, and bow. They were expected to live simply, to obey their leaders, and to kill themselves rather than surrender to an enemy. The samurai are remembered every September by a mounted archery contest. Horseback riders dressed as hunters shoot arrows at three targets, while going past them at full gallop.

Two of Japan's famous sports come from the samurai. *Judo* means the "way of gentleness." It grew out of a form of unarmed combat. *Kendo*, or the "way of the sword," developed from practice exercises in which samurai used bamboo swords.

► Yokohama lighthouse is the tallest in the world, at 106 meters (348 feet).

◄ *Kendo*, the art of fencing with bamboo swords.

▼ A *samurai* festival. Samurai were the Japanese warrior class.

Beautiful Mount Fuji

Mount Fuji is Japan's most famous mountain and its largest. Japanese people call it "Fuji-san." It is 3,776 meters (12,388 feet) high and an inactive volcano. It last erupted in 1707 and scattered ash as far as present-day Tokyo. Its perfect symmetry has always appealed to Japanese artists. During July and August, people are allowed to climb the mountain. The top is covered by snow for the other ten months. You will not need special equipment for the long climb, just strong boots and protection against the sun. It is especially rewarding to be at the summit at dawn. The sun rising through the clouds below is a wonderful sight.

Mount Fuji is in a national park, with the Five Lakes to the north and the Izu Peninsula to the south.

▼ Cherry blossom is the popular national flower of Japan.

▲ A bullet train speeds past Mount Fuji. The base of the mountain is 126 kilometers (78 miles) in circumference. A legend says that Fuji was created by an earthquake in 286 B.C.

▶ *Ikebana*, the art of flower arranging, is taught in special schools. The charm of many arrangements lies in their simple beauty.

14

The Five Lakes are ideal for skating and fishing in winter and boating in summer. You can take a boat trip across Lake Kawaguchi to see Mount Fuji and its reflection in the water, but the mountain is often covered with clouds.

Izu means springs, and there are over two thousand of them on the Izu Peninsula. There are also some special gardens, one with 5,000 varieties of cactuses, another with 35 different varieties of cherry trees which flower throughout the year. Japanese people very much like formal gardens. There are few gardens in the cities, but *ikebana*, the art of flower arranging, is very popular.

Two ancient capital cities

The shinkansen, or bullet train, will speed you south from Tokyo to Kyoto. It is the second fastest type of train in the world. There is a network of bullet trains all over Japan. The trains have an automatic braking system in case of earthquakes.

For over a thousand years, Kyoto was the capital of Japan. Kyoto became the center of the finest art, crafts, and culture, as it was the home of the emperor. Today it is famous for the skill of its craftsmen in making fine textiles, ceramics, lacquerware, and dolls. You can see craftsmen at work in many of the smaller shops and at the Kyoto Handicraft Center.

Vast bamboo groves surround Kyoto. Bamboo is a strong, deep-rooted plant that can even withstand earthquakes. Yet it is very flexible and can be bent to make baskets and vases.

There are more than 2,000 Buddhist temples, Shinto shrines, and gardens in Kyoto. One of the most popular is the Chion-in Temple, which has the largest gates and heaviest bell in Japan. It takes seventeen monks to ring the bell.

At Nijo Castle in central Kyoto, built in 1603, the corridors are set on special squeaking pins. These warned the castle guards if a stranger tried to approach.

Nara is south of Kyoto. At one time it was the capital of Japan. Around the year 400, the rulers of this area made contact with the great civilization of China. The Japanese learned the art of writing, growing rice, making silk, porcelain, and lacquerware from the Chinese. They also learned about the Buddhist religion. The Todaiji Temple is one of the biggest wooden buildings in the world. Inside it is a statue of Buddha. This is the biggest bronze statue in the world at over 25 meters (80 feet) high.

▶ Bamboo is the giant of all grasses. Many kinds grow as tall as trees. Bamboo is also one of the fastest growing plants. Some kinds reach a height of over 20 meters (66 feet) in six to eight weeks.

▼ The Gion Festival dates back to the 9th century. It is one of Kyoto's most popular events each July. Huge floats move through the streets.

▲ The statue of Buddha in the Todaiji Temple, Nara. Emperor Shomu had this temple built in 745. It took seven years to complete.

Centers of industry

Osaka has always been a center of trade. It became especially important after the great earthquake of 1923 destroyed Yokohama. A quarter of all goods manufactured in Japan come from Osaka. The businessmen of Osaka enjoy their food, and the city is famous for its restaurants. One of the most popular local dishes is called *Osaka sushi*. Pieces of fish or eel and rice are pressed into a wooden mold to make a delicious take-away cube.

The Yodo river and many canals cut through Osaka. Hundreds of bridges connect different parts of the city. Osaka is the home of *bunraku*, the traditional puppet drama. The puppets are about two-thirds life-size and are worked by three masked operators. It can take about 30 years to become an expert puppeteer. Osaka is also famous for its castle. It was built 400 years ago for Hideyoshi Toyotomi to show his great power. Most of the castle today is a copy, as the original was destroyed by war, fires, and lightning.

A short railway journey will take you to Kobe, Japan's busiest port. Kobe beef is an expensive delicacy. Kobe is a major industrial city, with big shipyards and machinery plants. Foreign trade is important for Japan, as it has few supplies of energy or raw materials of its own. Japan has to import almost all of its oil and metals, wood and wood pulp, and about a quarter of its food. To pay for these, Japan makes a wide range of cars and electrical goods, such as televisions and videocassette recorders, and sells them abroad.

You can take a fully computerized, driverless monorail to Port Island. The island is artificial and built in Kobe harbor. There is a fine view of the city from the tower on the island.

18

◄ A view over the skyscrapers to Kobe harbor. The port serves 10,000 ships a year. They bring in cargoes of raw cotton, wool, steel, and coal. They take out huge quantities of rubber products, chemicals, textiles, and canned goods.

◄ Japan makes more cars than any other country except the U.S.A. Japanese cars, and Japanese work methods, have become famous throughout the world.

► *Bunraku* puppets look almost human, when they dance, fight, laugh, and cry. The master puppeteer controls the puppet's head and right hand. He has two assistants.

The smallest main island

A boat from Kobe travels across the Harima Sea to Takamatsu, a city on Shikoku. The journey takes about four and a half hours, and the boat passes many small islands. Shikoku is the smallest of the main islands. It is a mixture of old and new, like the island of Honshu. There are modern factories and industry, but Shikoku is also known for its 88 temples which honor a priest called Kukai. Kukai helped to bring Buddhism from China, and he invented the Japanese alphabet, called *hiragana*.

Japan has two main religions. The oldest is Shinto, which is found only in Japan. It is based on respect for nature. The other is Buddhism, which originated in India, and came to Japan through China. Buddhists believe in the duty of kindness to all living things. Most Japanese people are followers of both Shinto and Buddhism. Religion is less important in daily life than it once was, but many Japanese people visit a holy place on New Year's Day and enjoy the many traditional festivals. Shikoku has the Hot Spring Festival in March, when people parade in fancy dress, and the Odori in August, when they sing and dance in the streets.

As you travel around Japan, you will probably see children in uniform on their way to and from school. Japanese children work very hard at school, and many go to evening classes for extra lessons. Japanese writing is very difficult to learn, but nearly everybody can read and write. As Japan has very few natural resources, it depends on the skill and hard work of its people for its wealth.

► A Shinto wedding ceremony. The bride wears a special wedding kimono and a white band on her head.

▲ Japanese children do their schoolwork with a pencil or pen. They also learn to write gracefully with a brush and ink. This is called *calligraphy*.

▼ Children have lunch on a school outing to the zoo.

Kyushu

You can take a ferry from Shikoku to Kyushu, the southernmost of the four main islands of Japan. Kyushu was the first part of Japan to be influenced by the rest of the world. 700 years ago, Kublai Khan led a fleet of Mongol warriors to attack Kyushu, but a typhoon destroyed the fleet and saved Japan from invasion. Portuguese, Dutch, and Spanish ships arrived about 300 years ago, but until 1859 they were not allowed beyond an island in the harbor of Nagasaki. Even so, ideas and goods from Europe reached Nagasaki, which became a center for trade and European learning. Today there is a strong feeling of the past in Kyushu.

A bus ride across Kyushu will show you the old Japan. You can start at Beppu, which is a town with many hot springs. You will see people walking about the town in cotton kimonos after bathing in the springs. In Japanese hotels, guests often share large communal baths. Guests always soap and rinse themselves before they get into the bath, where they relax in very hot water.

As you travel to nearby Mount Aso, you pass through wonderful green countryside of rice fields and bamboo groves. Japan grows enough rice to feed all its people. One of the craters of Mount Aso is still active. You can walk to its edge and hear the rumbling volcano and see the billowing smoke.

When you arrive at Kumamoto, you will see avenues lined with trees. The city has a beautiful old landscaped garden, in which there is a teahouse. There you can sip green tea called *ocha*, sitting on a straw mat and admiring the wonderful view.

A visit to Kyushu is a tour of Japan's past. The island is no longer the center of power, and town houses have not been replaced by skyscrapers.

▼ The Japanese tea ceremony is very formal and peaceful. The hostess makes tea according to traditional rules. The guest admires the beauty of the cup, sips the green tea, and eats a sweet.

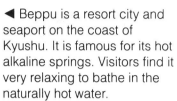

◄ Beppu is a resort city and seaport on the coast of Kyushu. It is famous for its hot alkaline springs. Visitors find it very relaxing to bathe in the naturally hot water.

▲ Rice seedlings are planted in flooded fields during the rainy season. This precious grain is grown on every piece of available land.

The west coast of Honshu

Hiroshima is known throughout the world. On August 6, 1945, near the end of the Second World War, an American plane dropped an atomic bomb on the city. Three days later, a second bomb was dropped on Nagasaki, on Kyushu island. August 6th is still the most solemn day of the year in Hiroshima. Buddhist, Christian, and Shinto services are held in the Peace Memorial Park to remember the dead.

From Hiroshima, you can take a train up the west coast of Honshu. As you travel north, you leave behind the industrial cities and seem to step back in time. Here you will find old-fashioned villages where people still live by fishing, forestry, and farming.

Many people from the cities go to Tohoku, the northern part of Honshu, for their holidays. They stay in a *ryokan*, a traditional Japanese inn. When you go inside, you take off your shoes and put on slippers, as you would in a Japanese home. You stay in a plain room with *shoji*, which are sliding paper walls.

▲ Children visit the Peace Memorial Park in Hiroshima.

► There is not very much flat land in Japan. In the valleys, farming villages are surrounded by flooded rice fields and forests. The farmers use as much of the land as possible. Some farming is still done by hand, but most farmers use modern tractors and equipment.

Tatami, or straw mats, will be on the floor. There may be a low table, some cushions, and a long, simple scroll on the wall. Traditional meals are served in your room by maids wearing kimonos.

Many Japanese homes have traditional and modern furniture. Most families have a television and electrical appliances, as well as a low table and straw mats. In the cities, most people live in apartments, often far from their school or work. In Tohoku there is a feeling of much greater living space.

▲ Most Japanese houses are quite small, made of wood, with tiled roofs. Sliding partitions with square paper windowpanes enclose the rooms. These children are playing a game on the family computer.

Hokkaido

Since 1988, people have been able to travel from Honshu to Hokkaido through the world's longest tunnel. The tunnel is 54 kilometers (34 miles) long, and has shortened the train journey from Tokyo to Sapporo by eleven hours.

Hokkaido's wide open spaces make it an important supplier of food and raw materials. Fishing and dairy farming are important industries, and potatoes, corn, wheat, and beans are major crops. Rice will not grow on Hokkaido, as the winters are too cold.

Hokkaido is the home of the Ainu, the original inhabitants of Japan. The Ainu used to live on Kyushu and Honshu, but they were gradually driven north by the ancestors of the present-day Japanese. In the end, they fled to Hokkaido. The Ainu are a tall, heavily-built people. They had their own language and religion, but now there are few of them left.

Sapporo, the capital of the island, is a very popular ski resort. During February there is a Snow Festival with ice statues of animals and famous buildings.

Traveling around Hokkaido is quite different from visiting the rest of Japan. It is the countryside that is most fascinating, not the cities. There are bears and deer wandering through the forests. The volcanic mountains are extraordinary. In 1945, a potato farmer was startled to see a new volcano rise out of his farm. Many of the islands off the coast of Hokkaido are actually the peaks of volcanoes.

Japan is an enchanting country, blending ancient tradition with modern technology. You could visit Japan many times, and still discover many delightful surprises.

▶ Sapporo is full of wide avenues and parks.

▲ Ice sculpture at the Winter Festival in Abashiri.

▼ An Ainu chieftain. Some historians believe the Ainu people came to Japan from Siberia.

Fact file

Japan's population

Japan is one of the most densely populated countries in the world. There are 326 people to every square kilometer (844 per sq. mi.) in Japan. This compares with less than 3 people per square kilometer (6 per sq. mi.) in Canada.

About three-quarters of Japan's population live in towns and cities. Japan has 11 cities with a population of more than a million: Tokyo, Yokohama, Osaka, Nagoya, Sapporo, Kyoto, Kobe, Fukuoka, Kawasaki, Kitakyushu, and Hiroshima. About 440 of the nearly 4,000 islands of Japan are inhabited.

Japanese people

The original inhabitants of Japan were the Ainu. Now there are only about 20,000 Ainu left. They live on the island of Hokkaido. The present-day Japanese are probably of mixed Malay, Manchu, and Korean descent. There are very few minorities. Most Japanese follow both Shinto, "the Way of the Gods," and Buddhism, which came from China.

An industrial nation

Japan is one of the world's most powerful trading nations. Yet it has few natural resources, and minerals and other raw materials have to be imported. Japan builds more ships than any other country in the world. More than 10 million cars and 5 million motorcycles are produced each year.

Japan is also a world leader in the production of calculators, pianos, radios, television sets, typewriters, washing machines, and watches.

Fishing

Japan is the world's leading fishing nation. There are about 450,000 registered fishing vessels. They catch over 10 million tons of fish each year. The Japanese also eat the most fish – over 3 million tons each year, or 25 kg (55 lbs.) per person!

The language of Japan

There are small differences in various regions, but everyone understands the standard form of Japanese spoken in Tokyo. This standard form is used in schools and on radio and television. Japanese words are represented by written symbols. Say it in Japanese!

good day	kon-ni-chi-wa
goodbye	sa-yo-na-ra
Japan	Nip-pon
thank you	a-ri-ga-to
one	i-chi
two	ni
three	san

Some national holidays

In Japan, January 15th is Adults' Day; May 5th is Children's Day; and September 15th is Respect for the Aged Day.

Education

All children go to primary school between the ages of six and twelve. From 12 to 15 they go to junior high school. They are allowed to leave school at 15, but nearly everyone stays on until they are 18. More than a third of pupils who complete senior high school go to a university. There are more than 400 universities in Japan.

Newspapers and magazines

Japanese people read more newspapers than any other nation in the world. There are more than 100 daily papers to choose from, and nearly 40 million copies are sold each day. There are also 2,700 Japanese magazines, and comics are very popular.

◀ Some of the 2,700 Japanese magazines, on sale outside a store in Tokyo. The children seem to be very interested too!

Art and drama

The Japanese value calligraphy – the art of beautiful writing – as a great art form. Japanese artists developed the colored wood-block print. One of Japan's greatest artists, Hokusai (1760-1849), made prints of beautiful landscapes.

There are three traditional forms of Japanese drama. Puppeteers train for many years to master the art of *bunraku*, or puppet theater. The main characters in *noh*, or masked theater, wear carved wooden masks. In the *kabuki*, or costumed theater, all the parts are usually played by men. The actors wear brightly colored make-up, especially those playing women's roles.

Sports

The Japanese enjoy taking part in sports as well as watching them. Favorite sports are: jogging, baseball, swimming, fishing, table tennis, badminton, softball, cycling, volleyball and tennis.

▲ A market stall is a good place to select designs and materials for a new kimono.

◀ A young baseball player in Yokohama. Baseball is a favorite sport in Japan.

B.C.	Time chart
4500	Jomon hunting and fishing culture; makes decorated pottery.
250	Yayoi culture introduces bronze and iron.

A.D.

300	Introduction from north-east Asia of rice-growing, horses, and armor; building of great tombs.
400	Yamato family become emperors.
405	Writing with Chinese characters (*kanji*) introduced.
552	Buddhism introduced from China.
593-622	Prince Shotoku makes Buddhism the official religion and sends first official embassy to China.
710	Capital established at Nara.
794	Capital moved to Kyoto.
1156	Heike civil wars begin as Taira family struggle for power.
1192	Yoritomo Minamoto seizes power as shogun, crushing Taira and making Kamakura his capital.
1227	Introduction of Zen form of Buddhism from China.
1274-1281	Attempted invasions of Japan by Mongol fleets from China defeated by typhoons.
1543	Portuguese sailors are the first Europeans to reach Japan.
1549	Catholic missionary St. Francis Xavier introduces Christianity.
1592-1598	Warlord Hideyoshi Toyotomi tries to invade China through Korea.
1600	Ieyasu Tokugawa becomes supreme warlord.
1639	Japan expels all western foreigners except the Dutch and bans Christianity.

1720	Japan relaxes its isolation policy by allowing import of books.
1853	Commodore Matthew Perry forces Japan to open to trade.
1868	16-year-old Emperor Meiji takes power; moves capital to Edo.
1872	Japan introduces western calendar and opens first railway.
1889	Japan adopts western-style constitution and parliament.
1894-1895	Japan defeats China and takes Formosa (Taiwan).
1905	Japan defeats Russia.
1910	Japan takes over Korea.
1912	Death of Emperor Meiji.
1914	Japan joins Allies in World War I.
1923	Great Kanto earthquake.
1926	Hirohito becomes emperor.
1937	Japan invades China.
1941	Japan attacks U.S. naval base at Pearl Harbor.
1941-1945	Japan fights against Allies in World War II.
1945	Atomic bombs dropped on Hiroshima and Nagasaki; Japan surrenders.
1947	Japan adopts new form of government; reforms education, agriculture, and industry.
1952	End of Allied occupation.
1956	Japan joins the United Nations.
1964	Summer Olympic Games held in Tokyo.
1971	Emperor Hirohito and Empress Nagako visit Europe.
1972	Winter Olympic Games held in Sapporo.
1989	Death of Emperor Hirohito, succeeded by Akihito.

Index